Life's Many Emotions

Vashni Kelly

BookLeaf Publishing

India | USA | UK

Life's Many Emotions © 2023 Vashni Kelly

All rights reserved.

Vashni Kelly asserts the moral right to be identified as author of this work.

Presentation by *BookLeaf Publishing*

Web: www.bookleafpub.com

E-mail: info@bookleafpub.com

ISBN: 9789358316414

First edition 2023

ACKNOWLEDGEMENT

To my children and amazing sister and brother who continue to support, uplift and inspire me.

Value

You have value in you, this is true, this can
never be taken from you.
Your persistence, your strength, and innocence
which is left,
Your unconditional love and acceptance of what
is less,
Your power, your wisdom, and courage pulled
you through,
Your sanity may be dishevelled, that still has
value too.

You have value in you, this is true, this can
never be taken from you.
Your skin, your hair, your complexion can be
renewed,
Your tangible differences will improve your
mind and mood,
Your need to be clear of negative deceivers,
Your encouragement to forge through to see
brighter receivers,
Your hold on life is stronger than glue, as you
have value in you, and this is true.

Warriors

We see ourselves as rising generations,
We are not meek.
We are not naive.
We are not alone.

We see ourselves as formidable lionesses,
We are not passive.
We are not disquieted.
We are not cretinous.

We see ourselves as virtuous humans,
We are not the immoral.
We are not the unjust.
We are not the incomprehensible.

We see ourselves as angelic creations,
We are not misguided.
We are not falsified.
We are not tainted.

We see ourselves as forging warriors,
We are not the perished.
We are not the forgotten.
We are not the defeated.

Black Diamonds

We are black diamonds in rough places,
Emerald rubies in tight spaces,
Heavy platinum, burned to the core,
Dense gold, gaunt and demure.

Silicate topaz, fractured and worn,
Parti-colored sapphires, broken and torn,
Metaphysical amethyst drawn to a close,
Sterling silver used and exposed.
Precious diamonds symbolizing us,
Retransform into shapes from grinded dust.

We are black diamonds in rough places,
Emerald rubies in tight space,
Chrysolite alexandrite illuminated no more,
Aquamarine beryl watered till poor.

Quartz citrine constrained and misshaped,
Semi-precious tourmaline, colorless and fake,
Abrasive garnet, separated until small,
Olivine peridotite decomposed till an eyesore.
Precious diamonds symbolizing us all,
Creating silhouettes to become functional.
We know who we are and where we should be,
We know what we want, including to be free.

As we are black diamonds in rough places,
Emerald rubies in tight space.

Blessed

5

The world today, that we live in,
Has evolved into something untold.
The hate, the pain, the dead, the insane,
Is all we feel, to hold.

Knowing when to shut it out,
And knowing when to cease,
Keeping hold of oneself,
Will effectively give you peace.

Be true to yourself,
Manage only what you can.
Do not allow negative things,
To shorten your lifespan's span.

Continue to be lithe,
Going only at your own pace.
Remember that you are human,
So give yourself grace.

Hold your head high,
For you should feel no shame.
Life is a rollercoaster,
And you are not to blame.

Although circumstances in your life,
Have not panned out.
Find new achievable goals,
To work on and dream about.

Divert your attention,
To rewarding and successful avenues.
Figure out what works for you,
And which route you should use.

Prepare yourself for great things,
Which will eventually come.
Once you have decided,
Which route you should start from.

In your own time,
Find out what comforts you best.
Always remember,
That you are well and truly blessed.

Time

Time was stolen, that cannot be renewed,
Happiness and success, something that's
overdue.
Bittersweet freedom came with a price,
You feel lost in a world where no protection will
suffice.

Betrayal and lies grind on your nerves,
Trust is a feeling few people deserve.
Greed and selfishness held you like weights,
Suspended dreams open the gates.

You cannot change what has been done to you,
You can only build on a brighter future for you.
Create something for only you to hold,
Continue to move forward and try to be bold.

Leave the past where it lies, see the world
through different eyes.

Words

What purpose hold these words, unbound
If actions echo, coldness found.

When greed eclipses all you share,
And hate's the cloak you choose to wear.

If time's a chain, if gain is pain,
When healings offered, yet you refrain.

When sadness breeds, hindrance in song,
And trust, a thread you cast too long.

When death's embraced, when mountains tower,
If love's redefined in darkest hour.

What essence in these words, it seems,
If actions negate the hopeful dreams.

Storm

Your life may come in waves,
Ride it the way you want to.
Your needs come in abundance.

Your mind may come as impaired,
Heal it the way you want to.
Your emotions may come in undulations.

Your healing may come through different
methods,
Pick the one you want to.
Your path may appear as listless.

Your learning may come as excessive,
Pace it the way you want to.
Your time may come as sluggish.

Your perception may come as emotional,
Feel it the way you want to.
Your understanding may come as diverse.

Your loved ones may come and go,
Grieve the way you want to.
Your moods may come as consolidations.

Your friends may come as foes,
Be wary the way you want to.
Your character may come as concealed.

Your emotions may come in storms,
Subdue them the way you want to.
Your personality may come as slides.

Cultish

Whistling winds, shadows afoot,
Devilish preachers, nooses and crooks.
Washed out lies, perils laid bare,
Deadly predators waiting to scare.
Desperate pleas, intimidating misdeeds,
Victims stripped like fragmented reeds.
Stained and smeared, bruises appear,
Cultish behaviour kept us here.

Dangerous games, unspoken crimes,
Dreams in flames, chilling times.
Un-watered seeds, selfishness with greed,
Shattered hearts that burn and bleed.
Fraudulent ways, battered like strays,
Dishonest customs amassed in parades.
Intrusive stares, nobody cares,
Cultish behaviour kept us here.

Terrifying actions, numerous infractions,
Startling behaviour, waiting for a saviour.
Starved of affection, no sense of direction,
Wounds unhealed displaying infections.
Fallen positions, hurtful admissions,
Attempting to fool like dark magicians.
Losing ideas, sadness for years,

Cultish behaviour kept us here.

Lost hopes, distressing gropes,
Caste out requests, ignorance unaddressed.
Negative confrontations, abhorrent sensations,
Connections built with broken foundations.
Painful nights, endless tears,
Darkest hours, predatory fears.
Loose lips, freedom is near,
Cultish behaviour kept us here.

This is not the end

Don't see it as the end,
When bad things happen in your life.

Don't feel like you can't win,
When you come across trouble and strife.

Don't think that you can't do,
When obstacles are in your path.

Don't believe that you can't achieve,
When others turn on you and laugh.

Don't act like you don't know,
When progression starts to show.

Don't forget the way to go,
When you're pushed from two to throw.

Don't see yourself as broken,
When others hurt you and leave wounds open.
Don't feel as if you're torn,
When lovers use you until you're worn.

Don't think to take your life,
When horrors imprint on you like a sharp knife.

Don't believe you're better off gone,
When everything in your life goes wrong.

Don't act like you can't move on,
When people leave you fighting to stay strong.

Don't forget you will always live long,
When all these things are dead and gone

Complacency

Complacency is working hard for nothing or
little to no rewards,
Navigating a work environment as if you're on a
chessboard,
Paving a way for others to succeed for
something they have not earned,
People downgrading your achievements, which
makes you feel burned.

It's essential to rid yourself of complacency,
So you can plan your life as you intended it to
be.
It's essential to rid yourself of complacency,
So that you can achieve what you deserve so
gratefully.

Complacency is matrimonial sex, which is
unpleasing with lovers,
Suffering in emotional silence while supporting
ungrateful others,
Giving your all in a relationship and receiving
nothing in return,
Showering your loved ones with affection as
they claw at your heart like a quern.

It's imperative to rid yourself of complacency,
So you can pave your life as you intended it to
be.
It's imperative to rid yourself of complacency,
So that you can achieve what you deserve so
gratefully.

Complacency is tolerating verbal violence,
which leads to your distress,
Being physically used and abused as if you're
nothing or less,
Continuing to remain and endure toxic
situationships,
Knowing that it will leave you broken and torn
and emotionally striped.

It is vital to rid yourself of complacency,
So you can plan your life as you intended it to
be.
It is vital to rid yourself of complacency,
So that you can achieve what you deserve so
gratefully.

Complacency is being at the bottom when you
know you deserve the top,
Being pushed and feeling pain which you know
you want to stop,
Playing complacent when you know you have a
voice,

Allowing others to decide when you know you
have a choice.

It is paramount to rid yourself of complacency,
So you can pave your life as you intended it to
be.
It is paramount to rid yourself of complacency,
So that you can achieve what you deserve so
gratefully.

Circumstances

Your being's not confined by fate,
Circumstances won't seal your state.
They try to grip, to hold you tight,
Yet within, strength fuels your flight.

Life's conditions, a tricky play,
They attempt to block your way,
But you, with power, can decide,
To soar, to conquer, to abide.

Within you lies the strength to weave
A tale anew, in which you believe.
Your story's script, yours to reclaim,
To transform, to conquer to end the game.

Control resides within your grasp,
No others hold, no shadows cast.
Troubles and strife, when they appear,
Your choice to face, without any fear.

Guide your will, be gentle, still,
Assess, adapt, against the chill.
Circumstances bend to your decree,
Less treacherous, a brighter spree.

Your world's reaction, yours to mould,
Negativity, its grasp you try to hold.
Evolve towards positivity's glow,
Your circumstances bloom and grow.

Reject the dark, embrace the light,
Sow seeds for a future bright.
Your needs align, your path you heed,
Circumstances, by you, decreed.

Courage

Courage to fight, to strive, to win,
Courage within your own skin.

For the beauty that you truly are,
Courage to thrive, to journey far.

Venture on with courage, hold it tight,
When others depart into the night.

Embrace new things, with courage, take wing,
Witness life's varied offerings it brings.

Courage to feel, to cherish oneself,
To embrace mental health, safeguard the wealth.

Know your essence, courage, it's your guide,
In strength, you stand, your power amplified.

My Love

My love, my all, heartbeat and soul's retreat,
In myriad reasons, my heart finds its beat.
You swallow my pain with love untamed,
Gratification and trust, in my soul, you've
claimed.

Extra miles, you traverse for my every need,
Walking the paths to fulfill my greed.
Anchor in the tempest when lost at sea,
Empowering me, tall as a tree.

You fuel my life's passions, spur my growth,
Respect showered, for you, my oath.
In struggles, new ways you deftly unpin,
Days broken, you're the light within.

Your love, a defining, insightful blend,
Hope and true love, anew, they transcend.
My love, your hope, a beacon bright,

Give yourself something.

In moments lost within a cloud's embrace,
Don't surrender, don't fade in that space.
When the world that is heavy, keeps pulling you
down,
Give yourself credit for this far-reaching ground.

Praise your journey, discovering who you are,
Amidst the chaos, amidst the scar.
Don't punish yourself for the past's deranged
maze,
Grant yourself time, at your own pace, to raise.

Healing unfolds in its own tender time,
Life's not a race, it's a rhythm, a rhyme.
Don't expect perfection in life's intricate brew,
Nor pure honesty in everyone you view.

Acquire the wisdom to start anew, bright,
Knowledge to guide through the darkest night.
Don't believe you won't traverse this road,
Or see life anew, in a different code.

You're stronger than you think, within your
soul's glow,
A break to regroup, to let your resilience show.
So, give yourself grace amidst this ebb and flow,

To breathe, to grow, to learn, to know.

Shed the negativity!

Deep within, the pain you hold,
Shame and lies, stories untold.

Burying them pulls you down,
Shed the negativity, let yourself rebound.

Embrace the new with an open mind,
Yet wary of those emotional binds.

Know your essence, your inner guide,
No longer taken on rides, where trust was
denied.

Patience is key as you navigate through,
Slow learning curves, growth ensues.

Deep within, the pain you hide,
Shame and lies, set them aside.

For they'll only drag you down and low,
Break free from negativity's dark shadow.

Innovate, but guard your heart,
Strings they pull, tearing apart.

Find yourself in depths inside,
No longer in others' tides to ride.

25

Time, a friend to learn and grow,
Patience, your ally in this flow.

Deep within, the pain you hold,
Shame and lies, stories untold.

But burying them pulls you down,
Shed the negativity, let yourself rebound.

No Regrets

I care not what your eyes perceive,
Your thoughts, opinions, I won't receive.
Pass me by on the street so fine,
Your gaze won't alter what's already mine.

Whispers pass, but I won't sway,
Fazed not by what you may say.
Pretend to care, feign emotions' flow,
Unconvinced, false devotions' show.

Fake promises, I see through,
No need for commotion, that much is true.
What you see is what you'll find,
Harshness sculpted, yet unrefined.

Evolution, not my aim just yet,
Transformed by harshness, no regret.

Waiting

27

I've waited patiently, I know my turn will shine,
When hurtful feelings fade, no longer being
mine.

Days of new emotions, pure and bright,
With contentment, devotion in their light.
Moments filled with positivity, alive and free,
In sunny horizons, peaceful, silent glee.

Walking with liveliness, giving, being kind,
Mood settings shift, blessings to find.
Loneliness fading, hollow no more,
Good deeds, a path anew to explore.

I've waited patiently, my time will bloom,
The hurtful feelings fade, into the gloom.

Females

Women's rights,
Their voices claim,
Their bodies simply are not a game,

Censured and shamed,
Pain felt just the same,
Women can kill, but
No longer tame,

Struggling, they aim
For love to reign,
Striving to rearrange
The world's unfair frame,
In unity, they engage,
To end the shame,
For females are always,
The one to blame.

Equality they fervently preserve,
Denied what they deserve,
Once a chosen reserve,
Women, seeking to conserve,
Hope for friendship's curve,
Love, respect that they all yearn,
Desiring for more that they should earn,
For females now deserve a turn.

Life Threw Me

Life tossed me limes,
I harnessed their zest to aid.
Life showed me signs,
Transformed them into lemonade.
Life offered hate,
I responded with love's glow.
Life revealed dark fate,
I faced it, not letting it grow.

Life hurled challenges,
But I stood tall, I didn't retreat.
Life brought the devil,
Yet I strived, refusing defeat.
Life curved its course,
That I never thought I could overcome.
Life tested with abuse's force,
I triumphed, until I won.

Freedom

Freedom stands tall facing evil's stare,
Don't falter, don't yield, their end laid bare.

Know your worth amidst their cruel deeds,
Rising high while their downfall speeds.

Courage to speak, seek aid, ask for care,
Even if fear whispers, even if they don't hear.

Your life, not filth, deserving humane grace,
Empowerment in knowledge to erase.

Live to thrive, not just to breathe,
Existence beyond mere days to seethe.

You're exceptional, beautiful, strong and free,
Embrace this truth, let your spirit be.

Inner Wealth

31

Navigating paths, distinguishing friend from foe,
Exploring beyond hidden doors, seeking causes
to know.

Comprehending morals, discerning right from
wrong,
Acknowledging when to depart, to a new place
to belong.

Choosing love over hate, kindness over disdain,
Opting not to cause harm, to shield from pain.

Hunting happiness, unravelling life's clues,
Seeking peace within, unveiling genuine hues.

Transforming into an authentic version of
oneself,
Metamorphosing dramatically to reflect the
inner wealth.